Sex

Love

GOD

&

Politics

...in the same sentence.

A book of Lyrics, Poems, Random Thoughts & Anecdotes

By

Luxe Crumb

Published by Michael Opera, LLC
ISBN-13: 978-0692643143
ISBN-10: 0692643141

Facebook.com/luxurycrumb
Twitter.com/ luxurycrumb

Created by Mike Glover Jr & William C. Moore III
Cover Artwork by Mello (Chanel E)

Printed in the United States of America

Intro

Sex is Love is God is Politics. We present to you a compilation of thoughts, poems and anecdotes to stimulate your consciousness and knowledge of self. We are all part of a phenomenally perfect world that gives in abundance, but also takes people, places, and things from us. We live extraordinarily short lives, however, there is a multitude of possibilities that are only available to you if you're willing to receive them with open hearts, minds, and spirit. We hope you enjoy these offerings and use them to unlock the mysteries and convoluted truths of Sex, Love, God and Politics.

1 Chance

1 chance 2 to keep you
3 words to tell you
more ways to show you I love you
1 chance to keep you within my reach
your gravity holds me down
if my world comes crashing down
like it could and it might soon
I promise to write you everyday
letters in a bottle
if the karma comes around
I would feel like you
I'm fighting not to
and hoping you're fighting too
1 chance 2 to keep you
3 words to tell you
more ways to show you I love you
1 chance to keep you within my reach
your gravity holds me down
if my feet were on the ground
I could tell you the feeling
But, I'm flying
your love leaves no ceilings.

You look better than cold water to a desert man

Oasis named Evelyn

Face comparable to angels
I'll attack every angle
To contort your expression
Into ecstasy and anguish

I've learned by reading your body language
How to fluently control your fluids
And to accurately identify where your pain is

Don't you believe for one second that love is painless

But remember the sunshine after the rain hits.

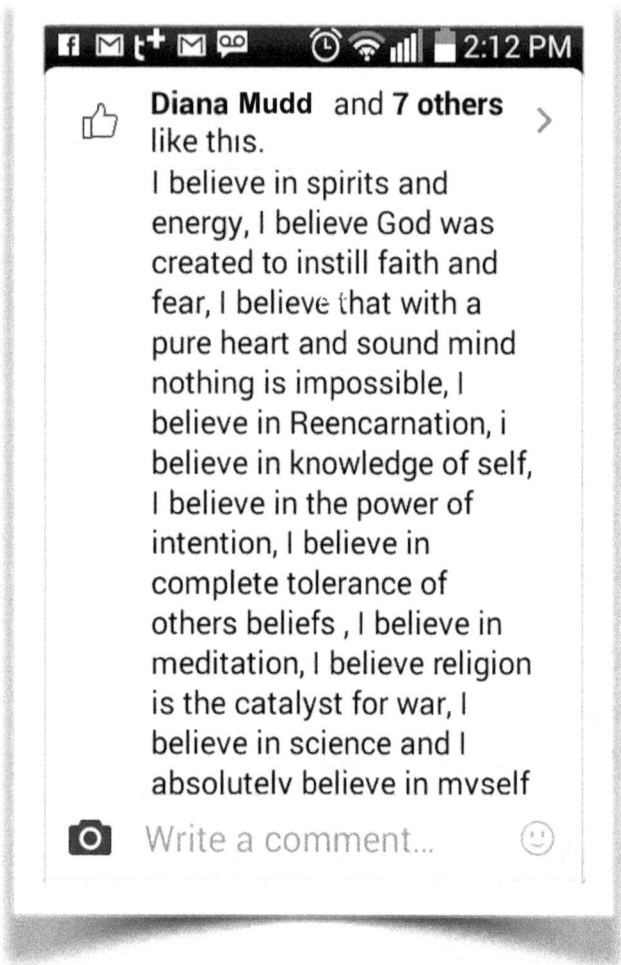

Diana Mudd and **7 others** like this.

I believe in spirits and energy, I believe God was created to instill faith and fear, I believe that with a pure heart and sound mind nothing is impossible, I believe in Reencarnation, i believe in knowledge of self, I believe in the power of intention, I believe in complete tolerance of others beliefs , I believe in meditation, I believe religion is the catalyst for war, I believe in science and I absolutely believe in myself

Write a comment...

Ya Sex

Ya Sex is national geographic
Graphic in nature
Ask the sky for a favor
Have 'em paint a portrait of
the body language we make up
We saying shit to each other that
don't deserve words or phrases
Just actions in cages
Our backs to the pavement
Rather, my lap is ya spaceship
Ride that to ya pearly gates
Fellowship with the saints
And compare me to a God
And just in-case they start to hate
Ask 'em, how could anything less than a God
get this far with a Goddess?

Tell em we'll wait...

I'll be loving you down while holding you up to the sun
Praying with you and for you
Debates in foreign tongues
Lakes that ripple and reflect the eastern sun

We stand still to catch a breather
While we bask in the light and our melanin gets replenished
I'm either the luckiest man alive or a dreamer
The most interesting man on the planet or just a cynical believer

I see us laughing under the moon
Engaged in war over our favorite cartoons
Deadlocked on how to be better people
We live in Love 'til the end of life and pray for an awesome sequel.

She's the kind of girl you get insurance for,
then watch your deductible soar.

😍 💰

Black out the sun

Black out the sun
Light up the night
Lay down your love
Open your eyes

I look up to God
He ain't so far from where we are
I shoot at a star
You wishing well
I'm wishing for
More loving than war.

My perpetually hard nature is indicative of my thirst for the intimate and your skin is an instrument that I strum... I just wanna hear the sound of your love, I want to feel the pound in your drum... I want to relieve you of your stresses and tickle you with caresses in the most sensitive areas on you.

I don't just want to be on you, but one with you. Intertwined into a symbol of eternal life. Let tonight be continued into the next one.

I'm ready to love you, until loving you is the only thing my muscles remember how to do. 'Til you lose control of your limbs temporarily, but momentarily you'll be ready for round 2. 'Til our souls leave these vessels and dwell amongst the stars still entangled in your arms. The inner workings of Love and God with no commercial breaks and a stripped façade.

Just you and I alone

My perpetually hard nature is indicative of my thirst for the intimate and your body is an instrument of Love... I just wanna hear you come, I want to taste the bliss from your tongue.

Albatross

Say you want to know how far my love would take me
Well...
To infinity and beyond
My ability and affinity for doing wrong is my harshest flaw
But for you, I'll lay my life down on a cross
My heart hopes you never get lost
More than on par I'm shooting for albatross excellence
When I approach you.

The very top and very bottom of this American pyramid are kin in greed, luxury addictions with unnecessary needs. Brands tagged and imprinted on the poor, insignias and monograms for the modern slaves and label whores.

But you go ahead and get yours. I know this can't be all that we are meant for. Men who bend over and touch toes for such riches and plush clothes. Diamonds that apologize for infidelities and fur coats...

This must be the Dark Ages, Sun's been clapped off. Everyday we walk outside alone in the dark, Ray Charles to the fact that we contribute a great deal of support to the inferiority complex we were taught.

Crux ta Circumstance

The political Crux.
Don't let them know too much
Give 'em conflicting reports
Until eventually they give zero fucks

Make sure their feelings about good and evil are equal
Propagandize the minds, Bastardize the people

The political Crux.
Printed on the dollar **"IN GOD WE TRUST"**
Remove faith from the schools
Don't even let 'em say grace over this lunch

But just to save face
Put a political figure front and center and
make him the grand master of the Easter parade
Keep 'em hopeful
Then launch a grenade

Love story, dead soldier
Stem cell research, ebola
Cops killed a nigga
Niggas killin' niggas

Across the aisle theres a peace offer
Watch nobody reach over

If we're at war
They're at peace
They feed this evil
So while we fight they feast

By the letter we follow what they instruct
So cross your heart
Hope to die
And believe in this crux.

Set of God

As the sun sets there are hues
of aqua blues, plum purples and gold.
Magical mysteries of God can
convince the coldest heart to unfold.

Beautifully Human

I bleed from the pricked fingertip
I touched the thorn
I lean toward shrill wilderness
But I belong

My skin is kissed by the Eastern star
My sun is the Earth
I reside on Mars
But I am beautifully human

I do declare
I love my lips
I love my hair

I hate my relationship with God
But I trust in his ways and I sit at his palm.

It is my Love

You can't stop my Love it wears number 23
It's Nashville Tennessee
It's the Capital before Katniss
It's the passion
It's a Hiroshima reenactment
It's tragic
It's magic
It's flagrant
Vagrant
It's a pre approved payment
It's coded in pre historic language
It's ghetto vernaculated
It's sacred
It's Oracle
The matrix
Rhetorically phrased sayings
endured fazes and pheromone lasers
You can't stop it.

 **Luxe Crumb**

I sometimes make up words like omni-purposeful but conversate is in the dictionary so to hell wit it.....#########**octo**-octothorpe

August 9, 2010 · BlackBerry Smartphones App · 👥

Attention: dumb bitch I went to school wit. as you may or may not know I am the epitome of Balance. this means I'm both the Gift and the Curse, Good and Evil , God and the Devil. Thus it is absolutely non productive and outright stupid to tell people that I aint shit. For this great Balance I possess makes me The Shit at the same time. This is not directed at any 1 person......no yes it is. I still can't lose Hoe

👍 Like   💬 Comment   ➤ Share

2 people like this.

u just went in ....lol
August 9, 2010 · Like

And out simultaneously
August 9, 2010 · Like

Wailing Siren

I hear the cry from the siren. She wails out a scream that could bring the whales out. I sail out to acknowledge her. And put my weight on her since she brings the scales out. She needs to be loved for a nautical mile. I release an inaudible growl as we hit waves. Wave runners zip past our face. My hands rest at her waist. My lips on her Virginia. Her mind's in outer space. She's here to take me away from the stress of the day. With a warm caress and a pound of cake.

I'm down to take swimming lessons in everyone of her Lakes. I'm proud to say I could smell her fragrance from two towns away. Put two crowns away, for Poseidon and his rider. When we get back from this voyage I'll sit right there beside her. With a healthy amount of enamel showing how happy I am just to float in her ocean. Her Mid-Atlantic deserves my devotion. Amid frantic clashes of calm versus convulsions. It just hit me. I wake up afloat because dreams come to me mostly when clouds are crying.

Snow falls in my mind.
It gathers into small piles.
Then turns into doves.

Dear God,

Even if you made me a bird
I could never fly away from here
I trust in your creation and your patience
To walk hand in hand with fear
To find positivity in the most negative probabilities
To handle blessings and curses with humility
While reciprocating the Love that was instilled in me
God willingly

God make me a beacon of hope
For the smoker and dealer of dope
For the uneducated and over regulated
Relegated hell we accustomed to living in
This holy ghost writer, blessed with your presence
I testify with my penmanship

God give me pure energy
And intent
Supersede the greed of the country we're in
Lead me to green pastures minus the pastors
Minus the passing of plates
I feel belief comes when faith is practiced

There's no salary that can shield you from reality
And no man can divide you from your individuality
We all struggle with duality
'Cause, balance is paramount
This is the way it gotta be.

The Times

love and war
fist and fuckin'
intercourse
bad construction
relationships
built on nothing
idiot bitches
dick for dummies
porn stars
pastor's daughter
internet, interfaith
in to faith
still into slaughter?
you into war, you fuckin' liar

niggas is roaches
hiphop church
Nas the preacher
holy ghost disperse
economist talk of big recession
but they ain't broke
turn the channel
Mugabe wilin', Cuba changin'
swine flu on Rikers island
gang bangin'
not in vain
politicians are dope in veins
astronaut, love drunk
crazy bitch
danger everywhere
in the food we eat
in the clothes we wear

look at my hair
is it jesus like?
if jesus lived, what was jesus like?
the image is flawed, the story is nice but
I don't believe in, mass deceivement

💰

Money On Top

Money is on top in a power stance giving long strokes to love.
Love is on all fours taking jabs to it's inner sanctum.
Now, after money is finished fucking you, thank him.

 **Luxe Crumb**

July 7 · 🌍

 July 7 · 🌍

Kings. Queens. Seems like people wanna be everything except human. But the only thing they are for certain is human.

Loveland

We've built this love on rhythm and soul
From youthful exuberance to skull and bone
Essentially in a world of unknowns
We've defined our divine roles
Leather and wood, granite and stone
We rock together forever to the jazzy tones of
saxophones

Syncopated rhythms and raspy trombones
Sunsets of plum purple, orange, and gold
Some circle the world to find what I got by my side
Adjacent to the throne is my navigation back home
In the era of lost souls you lead me to Loveland

You hold all of me in one hand

While balancing the world with the other.

I left my heart near Tennessee
In a state of albatross
I'll be better without it admittedly
I'm afraid all Love is lost.

Illuminum

Stand firmly in the light
Absorb its wisdom in sight
Express your passions in depth and
Love will Love itself.

Money on my

Money talks but I never heard it say much
Then one night I was dreaming Money was preaching
They were in a bar ritually drinking
A hundred, a fifty, and a stinkin' ass Lincoln
Benjie said to Abraham
"you never should have freed them
now they throw us out in the crowd and bitches be screaming"
Then Jackson intervened with
my niggas, is that not what the american dream is?

City full of dreamers
State full of funds
the filthy rich get filthier and niggas get none

Let some of my presidents represent me.

Black Church Burnin

A black church burned down today and nobody cares
There's a member of the clan dressed up as a messenger
He's delivering fear, death and terror
He believes in these endeavors
He was raised to hate, born to be wild
And will not let his country be overrun by
gays, blacks, jews and mexicans
He believes this country is his
and he believes this because it is true
His great grandfather's great grandfather
killed 1000 Algonquins and kept their teeth as trophies
Apparently aggression and brutality
are the foremost qualities needed to rule the world
With egos as fragile as pearls
And under evolved opinions are at an all time high
We can't be freed
We must free ourselves
And live, not survive.

Oreography

Faith is waking up in a black box yet, still dreaming of a white cloud.

🙏 🙏 🙏

Supernatural

May the fire stay ablaze
only comparable to the sun
And only able to be labeled
by a spirit thats unknown
It dwells above
It doesn't judge
It lives in everlasting love
It's the magical intangible
A perfectly balanced entangling of
Romance and God
With confidence, I call it Supernatural

Thought Afterthought

You ever been in the dark
waiting for your day to start
you just wanna see the light
feels like you're in jail for life?

You're actin like a damn C O
why you don't love me no more?
What did I do to get this death sentence?

I'm getting out to today
and I ain't looking your way
baby I promise
from my thoughts you are the farthest away

I need to forget ya
I'm not gon' regret ya
just act like that I never met ya

You're an afterthought

you ever put a car in park
then stepped on the gas
the engine just roars and roars
the car never moves at all?

that's what our love is like
remind me again why do we fight?
winning is a losing cause
we both end up wit scars

CHORUS

You're an afterthought

* * *

Good Man

I wear my sunglasses at night, to sleep and
shade the lights when they flash

> I hear the Sun's cry when I
> write

I feel the ray's heat and I bask
I tilt my face up to the light

> It felt like God was holding my
> hand

My vision cleared up for miles
and I saw myself as a Man

Life

we grew up in the slums, but we've come so far
and we are not defined by our foreign cars
from my hood to hood, or wherever you are
shine on you're a star, believe that

it's a beautiful life, don't you agree
I'm good as can be, because I'm breathing
it's a pleasure to say, I'm welcomed here
a smile's on my face, and you're the reason

love peace and war in a braided fabric
what are we fighting for?
still no answer
please don't all speak at once
usually you all talk so much
so we grind on and go hard
to buy our own lunch

it's a wonderful day, I'm happy I'm here
you can't get sick from what I'm eating
it's a beautiful Life, to Love is to share
I'll pour out my heart, if you need it.

Marijuana Gods

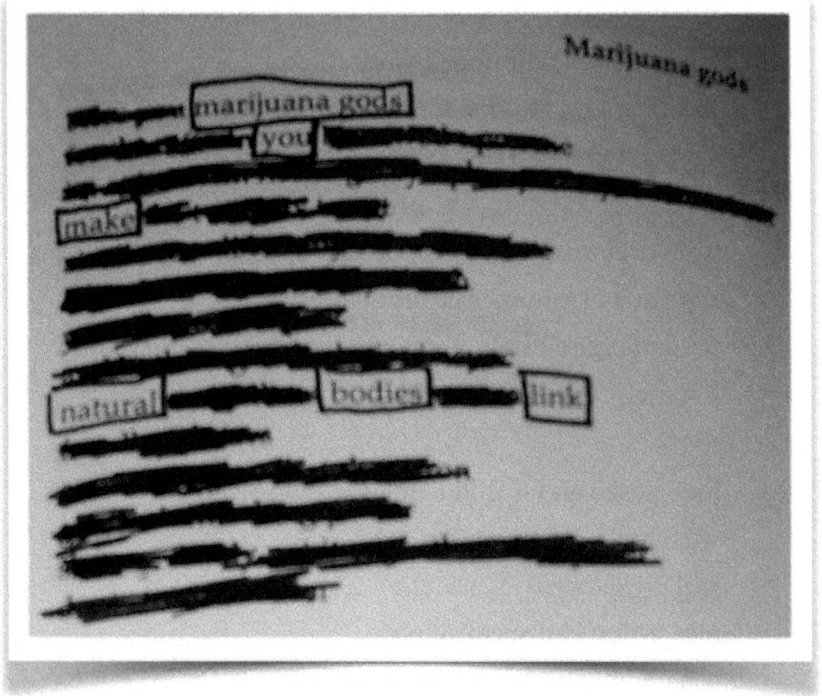

Run from love

I'm high off something different
most of my friends would think that its drugs
Something else got me lifted
sweep sweep my feet right off the rug

I used to see eye level wit the devil
but St. Peter's cool as f—k
I used to think the Gods were crazy
now I know they're just in Love

Thats why I run
I run from Love
can't have no fun
I run from Love

You've seen her previous devious
you see them chase her 'round the club
She like you 'cause you're different
her ex boyfriend is a f—king chump

Let's do the bump
let's bump these iphones
Lets do the hump
your lady lumps in my zone
voluptuous them thighs wrong (smh)
Baby they're so right, yet so wrong

That's why I run

I run from love 'cause Ima man
Her precious heart can't understand
Even if she stays, I know she cant stand it

That's why I run
I run from Love
can't have no fun
I run from Love

* * *

Everybody has relationship goals...but how many people are out there creating relationship itineraries? #EBLEB

29 Likes   1 Comment

○ Somebody   ○ Nobody   ○ Everybody

Ungraspable

This feeling that consumes us

And rules us

That may take us a lifetime to find

It manipulates time and space and minds

And has yet to be intelligently defined its just

Ungraspable

Laughable attempts at bottling it up has decreased it's value.

Klandestine

There are klansmen in the house of representatives
And they stand behind the opinions of white supremacists.

His Story

The manuscript of that man is history
May not ever been a manuscript
or plan in his parent's history

No more breath from his tongue
His lungs will never tell his story
to his daughters or his sons

Apparently, this opera get no rewrites
When that young man meets that young lady
late night for studies
The unexpected sperm donor
will have taught no lessons

The overseer misdirected
He holds the coldest blessings, with no gloves on
His life goes on. The other life, forever gone.

WORDS

And Bangers

I only have words to offer.... I trust you with the phrases

_____

_____

_____

_____

Oceans Away

You should just float along
And never look back
Nobody's at the shore
Waiting for you

I know and I'm sure
You're the storm
That ruin's the calm

Take off to a distant land
Break off these chains I'm in

Now we're oceans away
Worlds apart
Oceans away
So far.

If and When

If we are comfortable with where we are, we must be crazy
if we are hopeful for change without changing ourselves
we have to be kidding
it's been written for decades
generational folktales of where we're headed
and how glorious it will be when we get there
when are we going to this mysterious land of freedom?
is it here on American soil?
is it on the Mother land?
or on some space station in orbit?
'til then we stay dormant
addicted to normal, too good at conforming
not ready for life but making more of them
foams or Jordan's drop and we're all over them
job fairs, empty
simply there's no fairness here, no sharing here
the beast ain't hairy here
and we don't get married here
they don't want opinions to vary here
monolithic, anti-theistic, stylish n---as in Benz'
but IF or when we get there
Lets make a difference.

$ $ $

42

Long Way Home

I see you looking down but not once
did you reach to pick me up
Now I'm standing you cant understand it
I've landed I'm up

I could see you clearly walking down the short cut
so I took the long way home

My back didn't hurt more than my heart

Sticks and stones were thrown
when they threw my privacy out the window
and now I'm all exposed

My self esteem was gone
Like a streaming videos
you cant save me, no
I'm all alone

In this cold cold world
Just a lost soul beaten down to the ground
I got up on my own

I could see you clearly walking down the short cut
so I took the long way home

My back didn't hurt more than my heart

Over and again
more than anything
I remember me standing up
Never did I dwell on
times that I fell
'cause I'm standing now

In this cold world, just a lost
lost soul who's been beaten down to the ground
I got up on my own

I could see you clearly walking down the short cut
so I took the long way home

my back didn't hurt more than my heart

I took the long way home

* * *

Luxe Crumb

Smile for your storms
They wont last too long
The high tides will subside
Those clouds will move on

5 likes

👍 Like   💬 Comment

Box Cloud Contrast

In America you're either living in a black box or a white cloud
In that cloud you can see for miles
In that box the silence is loud
In the air there's a sense of freedom
But in here its all grieving
Mass deceiving
Lies and cheating
Rappers actors athletes and preachers
Represent the four corners that deceive us
With there boasted up egos and ethos of how blessed and
special they are to live life like a free throw
Man fuck them
They ain't black heroes

The black box taught us money clothes and how to freak hoes
All that from the words of our favorite songs

The white cloud taught them how to breathe and think free
From the skies they got a glimpse of culture
And they swarmed like vultures on everything we left for dead.

American Yin Yang

Black man don't know

White man don't show

Black man stay poor

White man make more

Black man be violent

White man be smart

White man make money

Black man make art

Surfs Up to Heaven

Oceans whisks away
>Scattered footprints from the shore
>Faith walks on the waves

Harlequin

I wanna live on a planet where everything ain't for granted.
Granted we're human and our minds vidalia full blooming. What in
the world are we doing? Crane falls, man dies, crane falls again.
Slavery, emancipation, slavery again. This time to technology, no
whips. Wouldn't wanna blemish that beautiful black skin. Mike
Jack made it black and white, his star shines in the black of night.
Go green for the cash in life. Cash that in for some solar power.
Roll one up for the hash in life. Magic imagination look to my sun
for my source of light. Thats my inspiration. This is for human
nature. This is for love. This is for the kids to breathe. I'm going
green.

Misses sexy picture post
I'll report this image
Not to Facebook
But, to my inner vision
Label it an example of Black Magic
Queen status
Every facet of your existence is existentially classic
Melanated skin kissed by God
Sculpted by the oceans
Backbone strong as 450,000 years of
Tears lost and swept away by the tide
I'm tired of your image
dominating my mind.

BMG

I need that
Jean Grae super witty
Cute face great titties
Lexicon hella smart
My girlfriend's Joan no ark
I need that Lauryn Hill Amanda Diva
Let me think uh I need that Pink
Bad Muthaf--ker

I'm just tryna find your love I'm Drakin hoe
Stay outta office on my Nixon throw the dick in
I say f--k the Hood bitches, I'm Reagan hoe

Prima donnas never prosper
Dumb dumbs cant double dutch and chew gum
You know multitask

Ima spaz if you don't STOP TEXTIN IN ALL CAPS
How you gettin' lost you ever heard of google maps?
Google this Luxe Crumb n---a
Fat like a bubble coat
Double quotations around "everything I'm sayin'"

I need a girl though on that Trey shit
with Chilli face but way waaay thick.

About her too...

This is a compilation of complicated relations
On a canvas of melody
This is loving you so aggressively
Some people may consider it a felony
This is my mind's recollection of ur passive aggression
The f--kin, the fighting
The love and the affection
This is everything I wanted to tell you but never texted
And my apology for being a creep
And having sex unprotected
This is a mirror of truths that's manifesting your reflection
Pointed it in my direction
Pardon my soliloquy about female friends you turned enemies
The rants about you not trusting
And the rush to judgments
Constant fussing, that's killing me
This is to make you aware that I'm aware that I hurt you
And to make it perfectly clear, this is a song about you
and a song about her too.

Dreams are No Good

Dreams come to me mostly when clouds are crying
and the angels looking down on me like they seen a demon
in my eyes but maybe they're all right I'm no good

Jessica's ugly, but not on the outside
Jennifer loves me, 'cause she thinks I'll be rich one day
Shana's a saint, really she ain't
but she would want you to believe thats she's great
they think they're great
maybe they're all roommates sharing mirrors

CHORUS

Leah's a nympho, in love with sexy time
Rachel's in limbo, she's gay but still does guys
Cindy's a bitch, really she is
but she would want you to believe thats she's great
They think they're great
maybe they're just sisters sharing mirrors

CHORUS

Anonymous

Mr john doe
Sir unknown
Why did u leave?
Why did u go?
Where are u now?
Show me your soul
We need the answers
We need to know
Martyred fathers and Sons
Mothers daughters
In love with the memories
Living life under siege
Patiently waiting for peace
but, misery loves company
I am not anonymous
My name is injustice.

World Be Free

republicans, welfare recipients and me
there is really no fee
to shower in the rain or bathe at the sea
near the shoreline theres a collection
of lost tears from funeral processions
with beautiful erections of the sun from the east
I pray facing there for reflection
with my back to the west wind
my eyes on the sun
and my mind on progression
if you're broke-back
you are not less than any man
unless he is God he cant judge anything
without first having faith.

Quantum

My perspective is a reflective light too fast to see
Yet clearly visible if you can see past the digitals
And live life physically.

***

Minion

I humbly stand before you as a minion with an opinion
A worker bee with no work ethic
Engaged in battles with commitment
Content with making more love than money
And an appreciation for existence
I humbly stand before you, cursed and gifted.

Lord Comes

Lord comes in mystery
Humbled in inequity
To alleviate the miserable from their misery
Unaffected by popularity and a tunnel vision of
forgiveness
Extended to those that bear witness to his wonders
When the lord comes.

Our Creator

Our creator was absolute and distinct in his design
Of the oceans, the plains and rain from the skies
Our weaknesses, strengths and fragile human minds
All combined to define
Existential sublime.

Ya Sex (cont)

Ya sex is classic, tragic, magical
Murderous traffic stops when we crash
Voyeurs pull out their phones to catch us
We make a how-to manual of what mammals do
Run it back in ya mind to admire how I handle u

Ya demeanor's a deceiver
Had me thinking u was a good girl
My father always said a shy girl better than a fly girl
Ya alter ego is a bad bitch
I could see it all on ya face
Right there where my hands are is a tattoo for ya waist
Ya Sex is ya Love
Don't let ya heart run in place
And since Love is a marathon
We gon' work out all day.

Essentially we are animals so when I see a women naked or dressed in revealing attire I respect the courage and bravery to strip away the fabrics that keep us out of sync with nature...ur birthday fits is fit for a King....Go head and fly free Naked Angel til u get your wings

👍 Like   💬 Comment   ➤ Share

To live by

Be good

Be smart

Be great

Be intelligent

Be kind

Be caring

Be aware of your heritage

Be charming

Be gracious

Be patient

Be true

Believe in yourself

Be sure to

Be You.

Luxe Crumb

Honesty is honestly modestly insulting if the truth hurts

PROJECT USA

It's all about you sir. There's no I in USA.....Bloods, white walls, and blue syrup. There's no me in USA, there's no we in USA, there's just you sir. Body resemblance of George Zimmerman with the head of Medusa. Mutated and aryanated, on behalf of the Rhythm Nation, what do you expect us to do sir?

It's a mighty fine afternoon sir. 5 minutes to 1, 2 hands up screaming don't shoot sir. At the mere thought of injustice we will loot sir. Because it seems like the black dollar matters more than black lives to you sir.

But anyway,

What you got for sale thats new sir. I need the 11's, the patent leathers, with the baby blues sir. And a pair of Japanese denims too sir. I'ma kill'em tonight all thanks to you sir. The bitches gon' be on me. The haters gon' catch the flu sir. Lord knows I love the haters, in the same way that I love you sir. See I receive the ether and use it to generate fuel sir. I possess higher levels of intelligence by the spool sir, and I've never graduated from your school sir. So no thanks to you sir, I'm an articulate, ubiquitous, cerebral lyricist, mentally militant, ambitious and ambivalent, but the money and the music goes through you sir.

So for U-SA,

   I'll call my brothers and sisters, niggas and bitches. Make em feel inferior to my materialism.

For you sir,

   I keep my head down and stay quiet about the truth.
I keep buying more things, and lying to the youth.

For you sir,

   I'll watch a lite-skin dude beat a dark skinned dude black and blue. Then with a sense of pride comment hashtag team lite-skin. You see I'm fighting my own ignorance as I write this for you sir. I write this for truth sir, for proof that we are cooth. For confirmation that our colloquial nature has been abused. So from now on I refuse to call you sir.

   I declare you America incorporated, where in a few short months another beneficiary of white privilege will be inaugurated. And, another racist cop is going to be exonerated, and CNN is going to televise the great racial debate with none other than Don Lemon moderating it. But I don't have cable, so I don't have to tolerate that s***. But my facebook timeline's hotline is gonna bling with ignorance and intolerance. They'll distracted us for 72 hours while bombing some foreign territory, then shower them with flowers.
#prayfor[your country here] but, who's going to pray for ours?
                ...You sir?

Theres a war

There's a war going on in the hearts and minds of the life bearers
The mothers are crying, their sons are dying, and the law gives
them night terrors
There's an eerie resemblance to public lynching, fire hoses, and
canine henchmen
Tear gas drenched us in Ferguson; we put our hands up in
remembrance.

There's a war going on in the hearts and the minds of the people
Our freedoms are compromised, our leaders are compromised
The teachers are compromised, the preachers are compromised
And we're still fighting for equal
"Those who are last will 1 day be first"
Is a pacifier I'm tired of tasting
My eyes awakened to the true evil we're facing
Waiting on the world to change it.

There's a war going on in the home of the brave
We're at war with each other
We are one in the same
There's a war going on in America
And, I'm afraid we're incapable of change.

Bluesy Bass Notes

Bluesy bass notes fill us
It's soul food for our chakras and nodules
Chicken soup for the soldiers of misfortune
who live through disproportionate ordinance
They're drowning you
You don't belong here nigga
They're uptowning you
Downing you
Forcing you and your kind to fit your behind
into this little box auto mobile
They're clowning you
Give your mother, your sister, and your misses
something to numb their menstrual
Dress you up, then strip you down
Show you how to minstrel
But our existence eclipses their resentments
444,000 years of resounding djembes pounding
Shake up the world and unearth the diamonds of humanity
Black gravity
It pulls us down to put us up on game that God is all around me.

That bluesy bass has been replaced by 808's and mental breaks
We really need to fearlessly reclaim our realty just for reality's
sake.

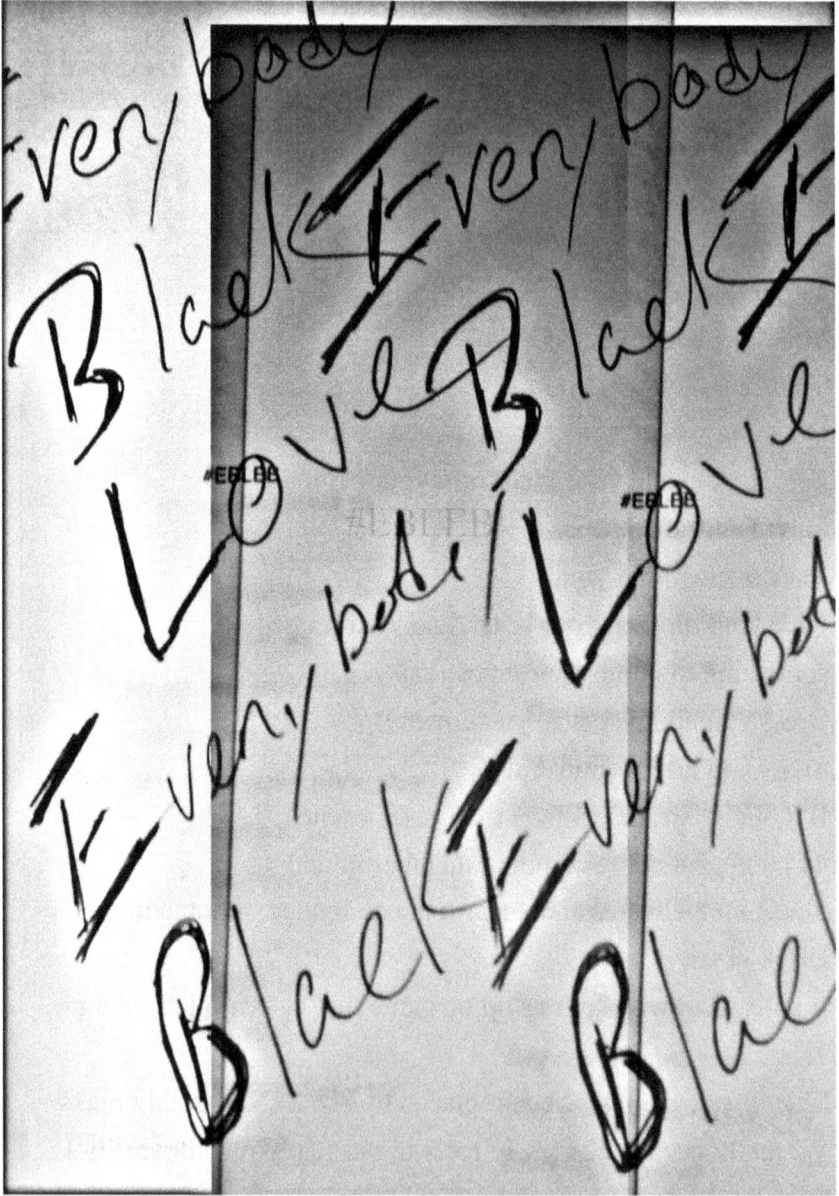

Same things

Same things that break us
gon' make us who we are
The same tree we hung from
Blood dripping
Strange fruit, steering wheel stain
Niggas grain grip it
Can't sugarcoat this

Trying to pull myself up
Stay down for my folks
Give 'em somethin' to hope for
Everyday I bless up
Every night Ima devil
Tug of war, no ropes.

Money Pop Fame

I want you to be better

, need you to see clearer

Beg you to listen

, not to me but to yourself

Trust in your conscience

, be conscious of that inner voice

It begs to be heard

, above the white noise.

Unplug your lifeline from the corporate pipeline

, we're not only supposed to chase money in our lifetime

When did happiness get subbed out for capitol gains?

Money Power Respect is now, Money Popularity Fame

Tangible Affirmations

I need tangible affirmations of Love

I want kisses and hugs and all of the above

I could scream at the top of my lungs

But the silence… soothes me

It pounds like a drum

Luxe Crumb

Sucking penis does not give you cancer......a husband maybe but certainly not cancer

Enamored

Do you not see this silly smirk on my face?
I'm enamored by you
If I can, I'll put the hammer on you
Put work in like a construction worker
Workin' overtime
Overtime you'll find
I just wanna be around you
I just wanna sway in your air
I sometimes find myself jealous of the wind
As it ripples through your hair
'round ya hips like a hula hoop
You are light years away from
The typical physical maze of amazing ladies
I've maneuvered through
You're just beautiful
Twinkling's of a silly little smirk
Perfectly perched on your lips and it's very cute
Guess you're enamored with me too.

Give Me Freedom

Give me freedom or give me death

Give me the Love of God 'til my last waking breath

Give me a reason to shake my regrets

I'm intrigued by the land and the seas intermeshed

Give me hope give me justice

Give me value give me peace

Or at least give me space

Just to Think.

The Pots Melting

As usual the confusion's in the stew
The roux is the news
the base of our miseducation
Bouillon cubes add the flavor
To trick your mental pallet
Make everything taste of syrup
Show them royals from Europe
Starving babies
Wild panthers from Africa
Niggers in America
And white supremacy for everyone
This jumbo evil gumbo
Steams up when they see us
athletic and hung low
The media like a Celebrity chef
stirring it up with relish and rhetoric

A word from our president...

A heavy serving of police brutality and irreverence served
up with impeccable presentation the plating is breathtaking
and theres still no justice for Eric Garner, So your honor,
for my crimes against humanity

I plead not guilty on the grounds of societal insanity.

Knights of the Golden Circle

We are all pawns on this chessboard
Tryna get across, get bucks like a horse
Knights of the golden circle on your lawn
Next to a burning cross
Searching for all gold everything
Fuck your confederacy.

Lord Comes

when yo top go back

and the sky turns black

and ya memories fade to grey

When the Lord comes don't cry like Aloysius

when the law comes better have no dirty dishes.

God is Love is Peace

God is
Love is
Peace is patience
patience is free

Faith is blind
Blind is dark

Dark can be light / if you are enlightened
Light can be dark

Ignorance is bliss
Bliss is peace
if peace grows impatient
Love concedes.

Luxe Crumb

I want you to love yourself as much as you love your wardrobe

#BYOV

When you look in the mirror tell me what do you see

are you as slim as you thought you'd always be?
do you act just like them actresses on TV?
and are you happy to be here with me ?

When you smile, thats the sun
when you cry, the world's gonna drown
in your eyes, I see Love
I think your beautiful when nobody else does

When you're looking in the mirror kiss your reflection
look in an upward direction
thank somebody for all your blessings
Be Your Own Valentine
Love yourself Love yourself

You're legit "As is" and you can't be replaced
God don't make no mistakes
Be Your Own Valentine
Love yourself Love yourself

CHORUS

***

#BYOV

Some think fat ppl are disgusting, some think skinny ppl are disgusting, I think superficial judgements are disgusting #EBLEB

32 Likes   3 Comments

👍 Like   💬 Comment   ➦ Share

Our Resentment

Why are we angry?
Why are we mad?
Why are we afraid?
Why are we ingrained with resentment?

Are we not America's children?
Have we done some heinous actions
    that warrants this treatment?

Does the melanin we possess
Make us less than?
Does the rhythm we exude
Make it easier to exclude us?

☐ Brains

☐ Beauty

☐ Sugar

☐ Sparkle

☑ All The Above

Kiss Away

I'll kiss the stars away
if you say you'll stay forever
kiss the moon away
don't need the light at all
I'll kiss the sun away
if you say you'll stay forever
don't know where I'd be without you
don't know where I would be with you.

Must Be In Love

so who do you think you are
think you can run
nobody runs from love
no matter how far
wherever you end up
you could turn around
love'll come around
and have you all tripped up

don't act so tough
go on let your guard down
it ain't gon' be easy
but nothing's hard now
live for today
go to sleep for tomorrow
drink up the love drown your sorrows

love then lose the love again
fall back in love again it's just a circle it revolves

it really doesn't matter not at all
the heart can feel the pain
but never understands the cause

when you're done with your fun and your playing
and you hear what I'm saying
then you change how you move
who you are, what you do
you must be in love.

* * *

Sweet Bitch

Luxe Crumb

Yo a few women I know are so sweet but then so sour.......pick a flavor bitch

Luxe Crumb

S/O to the dominicans in my building for singing
Stevie Wonders version of happy birthday......#**EBLEB**

Luxe Crumb   ⌄

If yall can't tell the difference between a satirical story
and a factual story how can you decipher between a
terrorist attack and a staged massacre?.........Ill wait

_____

_____

_____

_____

Karma Chameleons

My love for love is leaving, its coming to the end, the credits
scrolling slowly the light is a villain to the dark
KarmaKarmaKarma comes back to you hard.

But...
DramaDramaDrama's like snacks for the heart
We seem to love munchin' on utter dysfunction and washing it
down with
The most likely thing to drown in.

How then, do we refrain from treating bullet wounds with
band-aids and how do we stay away from the pheromonal
fountains?

Indecent

Contextually.......

You send the best texts

Intellectually.......

You have the best sex

and I'm pretty sure that you're aware

but Physically.......

I've never felt your caress

and Misery.........

is sure to manifest

if u continue to speak to me

Indecently.......

Lay Hands

Its 8:22 am on a cold Sunday morning and
the last thing on my mind is a sermon
I woke up reaching for you
worked my hand under the covers
Felt for you
I need your warm
My Ego melts for you
I'm vulnerable
hanging on by a thread swinging in the wind but
I'm sculpt-able
Make me your perfect man
In a world where love is lost
And lust is leading the league in at least 6 statistical categories
I'd sit at the end of the bench just for a glimpse of your aura
Your kisses replenish, your lips are like water
The skin on your inner thigh must of been inspiration for God to
create silk
I stand straight up to salute you, with not 1% of tilt
We run parallel to Heaven thru Hell
I see God in your eyes; I find bliss in your smell
It's now 8:46 am on a cold Sunday morning and
the only thing on my mind is
laying hands on you.

* * *

 **Luxe Crumb**

When my Woodchuck chucks I hope it carves out a
heart in a tree for ya love, I would go RnB for ya love,
climb to the top of a tree for ya love just to pick a
mango ayo Im in love

👍 Like   💬 Comment   ➤ Share

Perfect

you ever had a candlelight dinner
with the women that you love?
she gotta glow on her
and it's lookin' like its comin' from above

you ever stare at an angel in the face?
probably not, but anyway
you got a style you got a grace
you got the prettiest face
I've seen in a while
Just wanna keep you smilin' babe

People spend a lifetime tryna find
what I got by my side
People waste their time tryna find
the shiniest dime

I tell mine
baby you are
better than a model or a movie star
you're Perfect to me
you are Love

you ever made love on a cloud
warmed up by the sun?
you wouldn't wanna come down
trust me, you are not the only 1
you ever felt gravity gradually go?
slow? No?
Didn't think you did
baby I'm your Lincoln and
I give you the freedom and
let you fly back if you want to babe

People spend a lifetime tryna find
what I got by my side
People waste their time tryna find
the shiniest dime

CHORUS

* * *

Without a spray can or paint brush im still a basquiat.

fin.

SEX, LOVE, GOD & POLITICS... in the same sentence.

Thank You

Jasmine D. Glover
Ebony Moore
RiQ Designs
Chanel E
Phil Boyd
Osakwe Beale
Emanny Salgado
Riggs Rivera
BLUE

*Special thanks to our family, friends and anyone who has inspired these writings, showed us love, and gave us encouragement throughout our creative process. Your love has been paramount in manifesting this work.

Use this area to write, draw, and emote until your heart is content.

Snap a picture and share with us at #SLGP #LuxuryCrumb

Use this area to write, draw, and emote until your heart is content.

Use this area to write, draw, and emote until your heart is content.

✎ Use this area to write, draw, and emote until your heart is content.

Snap a picture and share with us at #SLGP #LuxuryCrumb

www.ingramcontent.com/pod-product-compliance
Lightning Source LLC
Chambersburg PA
CBHW071637050426
42443CB00028B/3353